BEGINNING TO END

Apple Seed to Juice

by Bryan Langdo

T0014984

BELLWETHER MEDIA · MINNEAPOLIS, MN

Blastoff! Readers are carefully developed by literacy experts to build reading stamina and move students toward fluency by combining standards-based content with developmentally appropriate text.

 Level 1 provides the most support through repetition of high-frequency words, light text, predictable sentence patterns, and strong visual support.

 Level 2 offers early readers a bit more challenge through varied sentences, increased text load, and text-supportive special features.

 Level 3 advances early-fluent readers toward fluency through increased text load, less reliance on photos, advancing concepts, longer sentences, and more complex special features.

★ **Blastoff! Universe**

Reading Level

Grade **K** → Grades **1-3** → Grade **4**

This edition first published in 2024 by Bellwether Media, Inc.

No part of this publication may be reproduced in whole or in part without written permission of the publisher. For information regarding permission, write to Bellwether Media, Inc., Attention: Permissions Department, 6012 Blue Circle Drive, Minnetonka, MN 55343.

Library of Congress Cataloging-in-Publication Data

LC record for Apple Seed to Juice available at: https://lccn.loc.gov/2023006497

Text copyright © 2024 by Bellwether Media, Inc. BLASTOFF! READERS and associated logos are trademarks and/or registered trademarks of Bellwether Media, Inc.

Editor: Elizabeth Neuenfeldt   Designer: Laura Sowers

Printed in the United States of America, North Mankato, MN.

Table of Contents

A Tasty Drink

orchard

How is apple juice made?
It is made from apples!

Who Grows the Most Apples?

China grows about 50 million tons (46 million metric tons) of apples each year!

Apples grow on apple trees. The trees grow in **orchards**.

In the Orchard

grafting

seeds

Farmers grow apple trees in soil. They plant seeds or **graft** trees.

Water and sunlight help the trees grow. The trees can grow apples in around 5 to 10 years.

What Makes Apple Trees Grow?

soil

water

sunlight

Each spring, flowers grow on apple trees. Bees **pollinate** the flowers.

The **pollen** makes apples grow. During summer, the apples grow bigger.

pollen

flowers

A Lot of Apples

There are around 7,500 kinds of apples in the world!

tree shaker

The apples are ready in fall.
A **tree shaker** shakes the trees.
Apples fall to the ground.

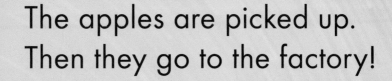

The apples are picked up.
Then they go to the factory!

In the factory, the apples are washed with cold water.

A **grinder** chops them.
Enzymes help break down
and soften the apples.

grinder

13

A **press** pushes mushy apples through a **filter**. Juice is squeezed out.

press

The juice is **pasteurized** to remove **bacteria**. It goes through more filters until it is clear.

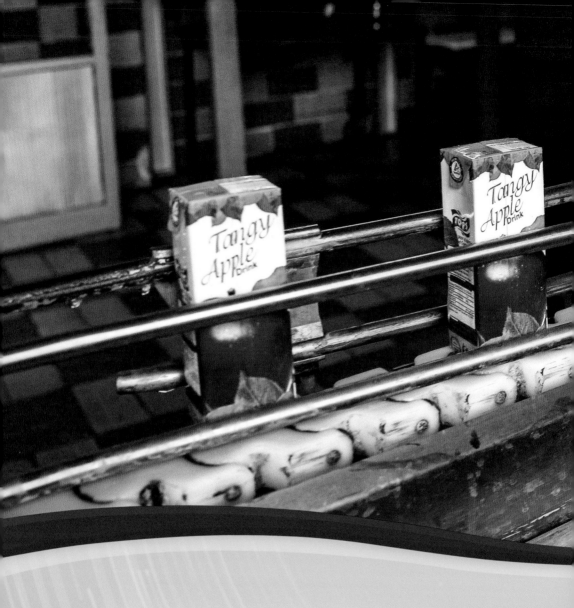

Small, clean juice boxes
move on a **conveyor**.
A machine pours in the juice.

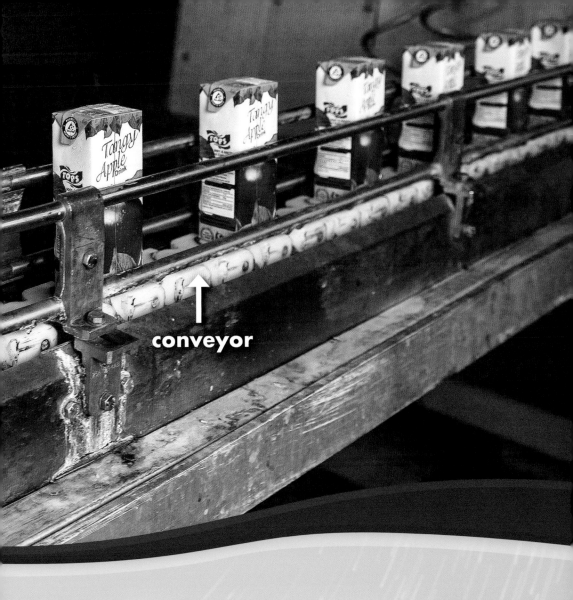

conveyor

Straws are glued onto
the side of each box.

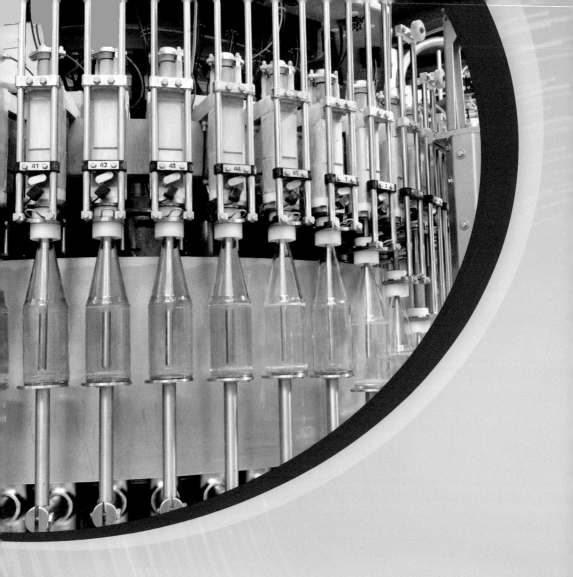

Other juice is poured into bottles.
The juice is loaded into trucks.
Then it is put in stores for people
to buy!

Apple Seed to Juice

1

apples are shaken
from trees

2

apples are washed
and chopped, and
enzymes are added

3

apples are pressed
to get juice out

4

juice is pasteurized
to remove bacteria

5

juice goes through filters
until clear

6

juice is put in boxes or
bottles and is sent
to stores

19

Some apple juice is in big bottles. Many children drink apple juice from juice boxes.

People around the
world love apple juice!

Glossary

bacteria—very tiny living things that can make a person sick

conveyor—a machine with a belt that moves things from one place to another

enzymes—substances that bring about chemical reactions; enzymes help get more juices from apples.

filter—an object with a screen that lets liquid flow through but stops solid things

graft—to put a twig from one plant into another plant so they grow together

grinder—a machine that grinds and chops things into small pieces

orchards—places where people grow fruit trees

pasteurized—heated and cooled to get rid of harmful bacteria

pollen—a fine dust that is needed to produce apples

pollinate—to move pollen from one plant to another

press—a machine that pushes down on something to get the juice out

tree shaker—a machine that shakes fruit trees to make the fruit fall off

To Learn More

AT THE LIBRARY

Amstutz, Lisa. *Let's Go to the Apple Orchard.*
North Mankato, Minn.: Capstone Press, 2021.

Colella, Jill. *Let's Explore Apples!* Minneapolis,
Minn.: Lerner Publications, 2020.

Kimmelman, Leslie. *Seed to Apple.* New York, N.Y.:
Scholastic, 2021.

ON THE WEB

FACTSURFER

Factsurfer.com gives you
a safe, fun way to find
more information.

1. Go to www.factsurfer.com.

2. Enter "apple seed to juice" into the search box
   and click 🔍.

3. Select your book cover to see a list
   of related content.

Index

The images in this book are reproduced through the courtesy of: studiovin, front cover; Sony Ho, front cover (inset); NIKCOA, p. 3; Vadim.Petrov, pp. 4-5; ATTILA Barsan, pp. 6-7; Santeri Viinamäki/ Wikipedia, p. 6 (seeds); Pinkyone, p. 7 (soil); Silarock, p. 7 (water); Elenamiv, p. 7 (sunlight); jamesvancouver, p. 8; trophyhunt, pp. 8-9; imageBROKER/ Alamy, pp. 10-11; Photoexpert, p. 11; Westend61 GmbH/ Alamy, pp. 12-13, 19 (2); Chala, p. 13; K_Thalhofer, pp. 14-15, 19 (3); aleks333, pp. 15, 19 (4); Bloomberg/ Getty Images, pp. 16-17; Industryviews, pp. 18, 19 (6); Cephas Picture Library/ Alamy, p. 19 (1); Andia/ Getty Images, p. 19 (5); Caiaimage/Paul Bradbury, pp. 20-21; Ohlesbeauxjours, p. 21; Nataliya Schmidt, p. 23.